FIRST 50
CLASSICAL PIECES
YOU SHOULD PLAY ON THE CLARINET

ISBN 978-1-5400-9709-5

Visit Hal Leonard Online at
www.halleonard.com

Contact us:
Hal Leonard
7777 West Bluemound Road
Milwaukee, WI 53213
Email: info@halleonard.com

In Europe, contact:
Hal Leonard Europe Limited
42 Wigmore Street
Marylebone, London, W1U 2RN
Email: info@halleonardeurope.com

In Australia, contact:
Hal Leonard Australia Pty. Ltd.
4 Lentara Court
Cheltenham, Victoria, 3192 Australia
Email: info@halleonard.com.au

CONTENTS
BY TITLE

FIRST 50 CLASSICAL PIECES

YOU SHOULD PLAY ON THE CLARINET

ISBN 978-1-5400-9709-5

HAL•LEONARD®

Visit Hal Leonard Online at
www.halleonard.com

Contact us:
Hal Leonard
7777 West Bluemound Road
Milwaukee, WI 53213
Email: info@halleonard.com

In Europe, contact:
Hal Leonard Europe Limited
42 Wigmore Street
Marylebone, London, W1U 2RN
Email: info@halleonardeurope.com

In Australia, contact:
Hal Leonard Australia Pty. Ltd.
4 Lentara Court
Cheltenham, Victoria, 3192 Australia
Email: info@halleonard.com.au

CONTENTS
BY TITLE

CONTENTS
BY COMPOSER

Minuet in D minor

from *Notebook for Anna Magdalena Bach*, BWV Appendix 132
originally for keyboard

Anonymous

Musette in D Major

from *Notebook for Anna Magdalena Bach*, BWV Appendix 126
originally for keyboard

Johann Sebastian Bach
(1685–1750)

Adagio
Op. 63, No. 24
originally for clarinet and piano

Carl Baermann
(1811–1885)

Schlummerlied
Op. 84, No. 2
originally for clarinet and piano

Carl Baermann
(1811–1885)

Marmotte

from *Eight Songs*, Op. 52, No. 7
originally for voice and piano

Ludwig van Beethoven
(1770–1827)

Minuet in G Major

from *Six Minuets*, WoO 10, No. 2

originally for piano

Ludwig van Beethoven
(1770–1827)

Tempo di Minuet

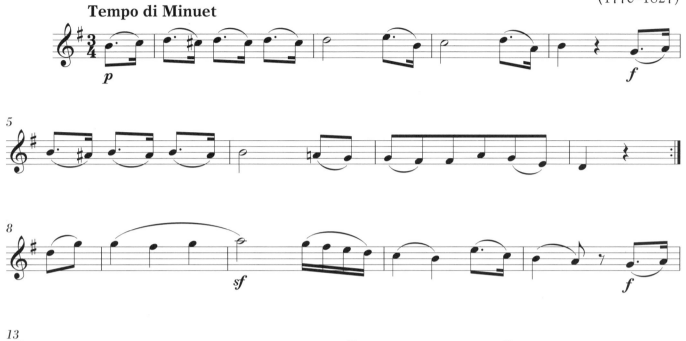

Ode to Joy

from Symphony No. 9 in D minor, Op. 125
originally for chorus and orchestra

Ludwig van Beethoven
(1770–1827)

Minuet

from String Quintet in E Major, Op. 11, No. 5

originally for string quintet

Luigi Boccherini
(1743–1805)

Allegretto

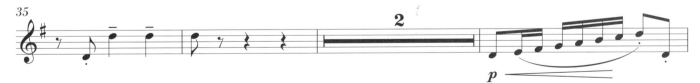

*Ornaments are optional.

Toreador's Song
(Votre toast, je peux vous le rondre)
from *Carmen*
originally for voice and orchestra

Georges Bizet
(1838–1875)

Hungarian Dance No. 5

originally for piano duo

Johannes Brahms
(1833–1897)

Lullaby
Op. 49, No. 4
originally for voice and piano

Johannes Brahms
(1833–1897)

Intermezzo
Op. 117, No. 1
originally for piano

Johannes Brahms
(1833–1897)

Un poco più andante

Waltz
Op. 39, No. 15
originally for piano

Johannes Brahms
(1833–1897)

Etude in E Major
Op. 10, No. 3
originally for piano

Frédéric Chopin
(1810–1849)

Largo

from Symphony No. 9 in E minor, Op. 95 "From the New World"

originally for orchestra

Antonín Dvořák
(1841–1904)

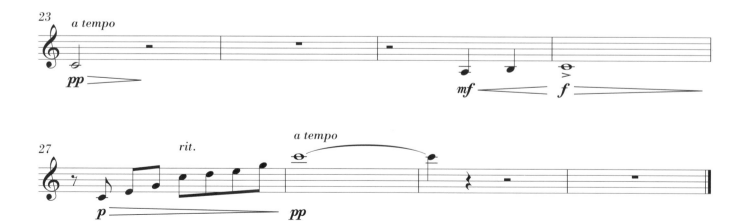

Pomp and Circumstance

March No. 1

originally for orchestra

Edward Elgar
(1857–1934)

Pavane
Op. 50
originally for piano

Gabriel Fauré
(1845–1924)

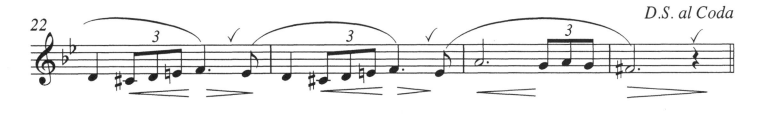

Mazurka in C minor

originally for piano

Mikhail Glinka
(1804–1857)

Dance of the Blessed Spirits

from *Orfeo ed Euridice*
originally for orchestra

Christoph Willibald Gluck
(1714–1787)

Funeral March of a Marionette

originally for piano

Charles Gounod
(1818–1893)

29

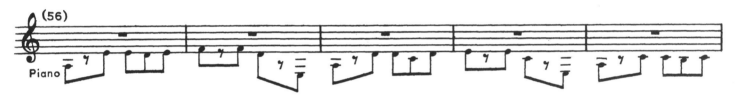

Irish Tune from County Derry

originally for piano

Percy Grainger
(1882–1961)

Solvejg's Song

from *Peer Gynt*
originally for orchestra

Edvard Grieg
(1843–1907)

He Shall Feed His Flock

from *Messiah*
originally for voice and orchestra

George Frideric Handel
(1685–1759)

Largo
(Ombra mai fù)
from *Serse*, HWV 40
originally for voice and orchestra

George Frideric Handel
(1685–1759)

Aria con Variazioni
from Suite in B-flat Major, HWV 434
originally for keyboard

George Frideric Handel
(1685–1759)

St. Anthony Chorale
originally for chamber ensemble

Franz Joseph Haydn
(1732–1809)

Andante

from Symphony No. 94 in G Major "Surprise"
originally for orchestra

Franz Joseph Haydn
(1732–1809)

Jupiter Chorale

from *The Planets*
originally for orchestra

Gustav Holst
(1874–1934)

Andante maestoso

Evening Prayer
from *Hansel and Gretel*
originally for voices and orchestra

Engelbert Humperdinck
(1854–1921)

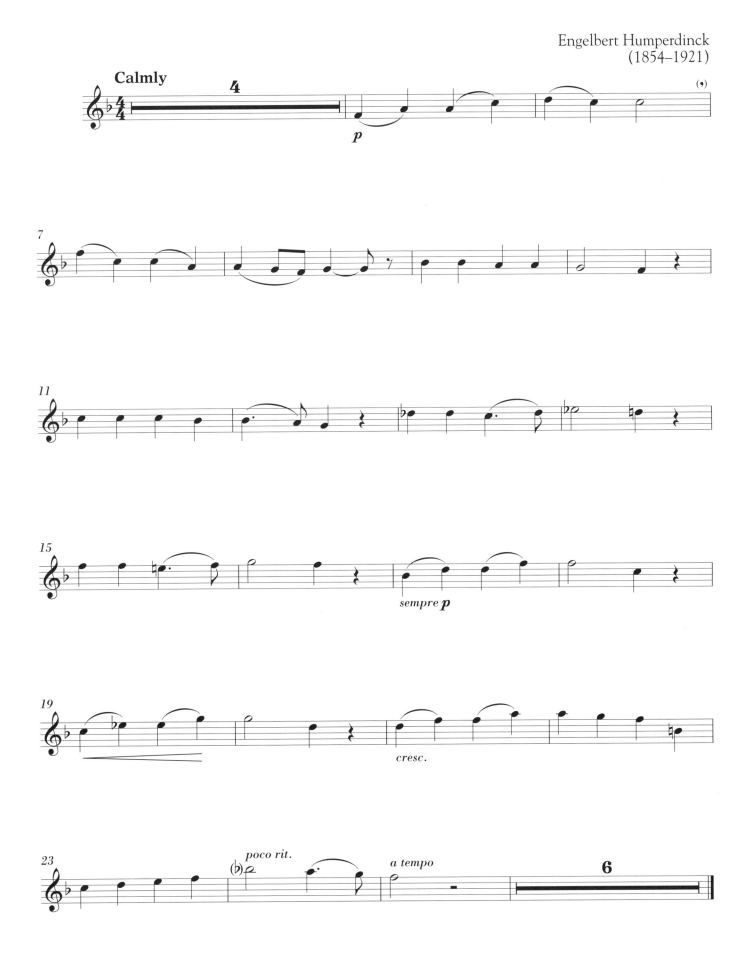

Waltz

from *The Merry Widow*

originally for orchestra

Franz Lehár
(1870–1948)

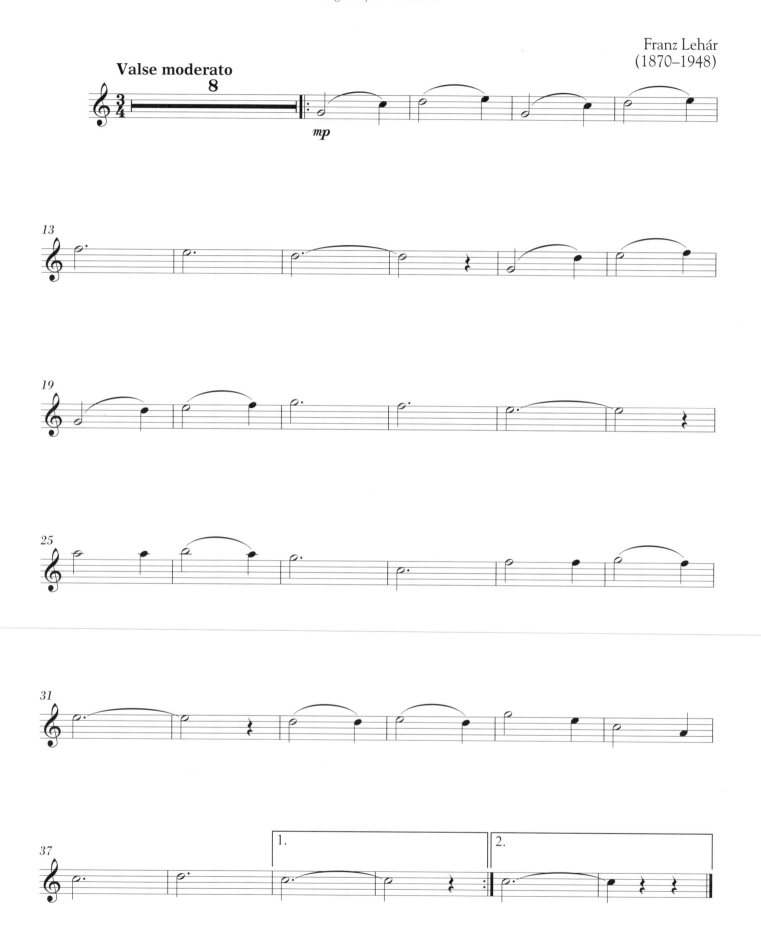

Barcarolle

from *The Tales of Hoffmann*
originally for voices and orchestra

Jacques Offenbach
(1819–1880)

Non più andrai

from *The Marriage of Figaro*
originally for voice and orchestra

Wolfgang Amadeus Mozart
(1756–1791)

Canon
(Canon in D)
originally for 3 violins and basso continuo

Johann Pachelbel
(1653–1706)

O mio babbino caro

from *Gianni Schicchi*
originally for voice and orchestra

Giacomo Puccini
(1858–1924)

Minuet in G Major

from *Notebook for Anna Magdalena Bach*, BWV Appendix 114
originally for keyboard

Christian Petzold
(1677–1733)

Minuet in G minor

from *Notebook for Anna Magdalena Bach*, BWV Appendix 115

originally for keyboard

Christian Petzold
(1677–1733)

Ave Maria
originally for voice and piano

Franz Schubert
(1797–1828)

Heidenröslein

Op. 3, No. 3

originally for voice and piano

Franz Schubert
(1797–1828)

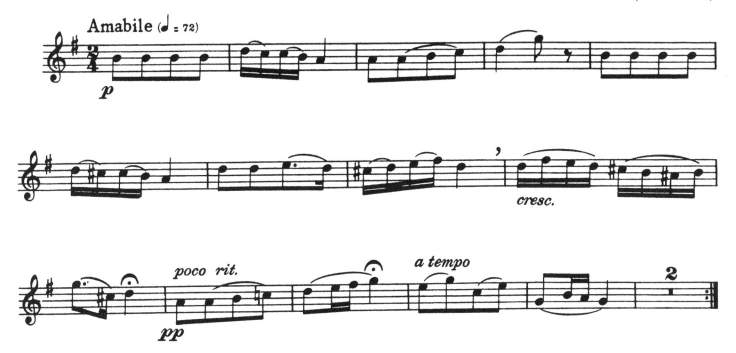

Lullaby

Op. 92, No. 2

originally for voice and piano

Franz Schubert
(1797–1828)

To Music
(An die Musik)
originally for voice and piano

Franz Schubert
(1797–1828)

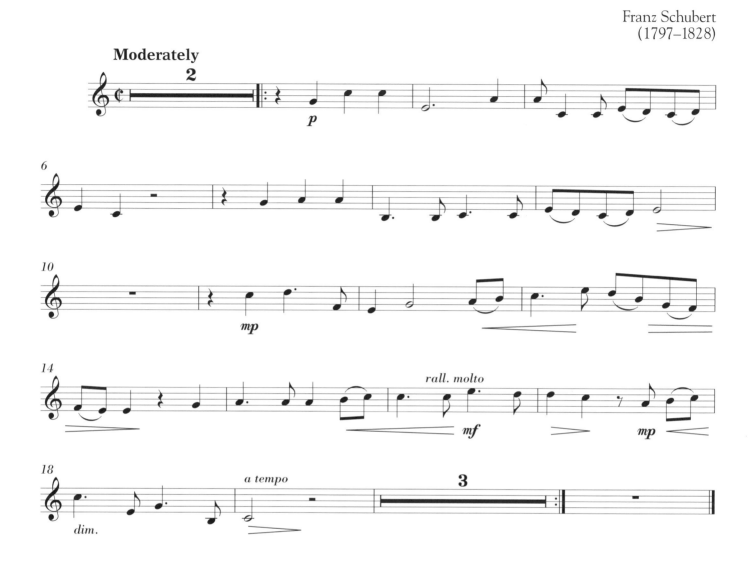

About Strange Lands and People

from *Scenes from Childhood*, Op. 15, No. 1

originally for piano

Robert Schumann
(1810–1856)

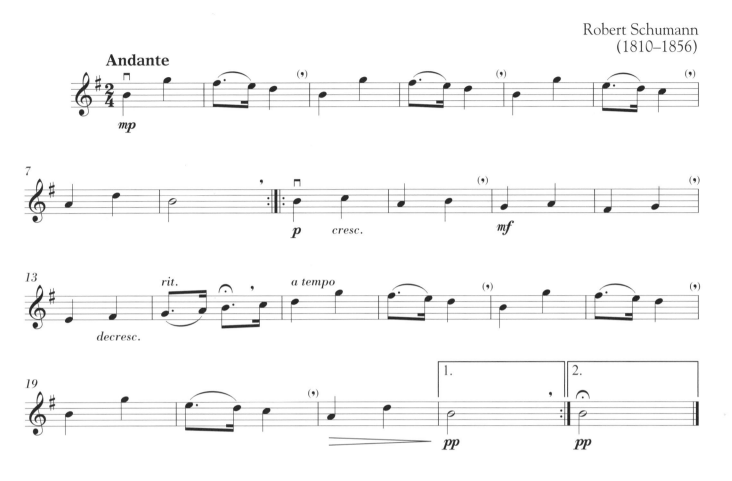

The Merry Farmer

from *Album for the Young*, Op. 68, No. 10
originally for piano

Robert Schumann
(1810–1856)

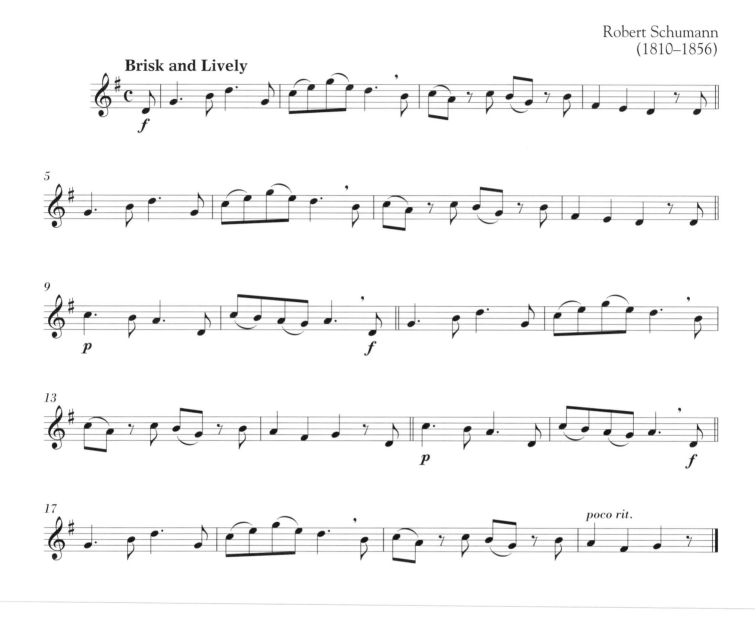

Wild Horseman
(Wilder Reiter)
from *Album for the Young*, Op. 68, No. 8
originally for piano

Robert Schumann
(1810–1856)

The Moldau

from *Ma Vlast*
originally for orchestra

Bedřich Smetana
(1824–1884)

Emperor Waltz

originally for orchestra

Johann Strauss II
(1825–1899)

Tempo di valse

On the Beautiful Blue Danube

originally for orchestra

Johann Strauss II
(1825–1899)

Andante

from Symphony No. 6 in B minor, Op. 74
"Pathétique"
originally for orchestra

Pyotr Il'yich Tchaikovsky
(1840–1893)

Theme

from *Swan Lake*
originally for orchestra

Pyotr Il'yich Tchaikovsky
(1840–1893)

Waltz

from *Sleeping Beauty*
originally for orchestra

Pyotr Il'yich Tchaikovsky
(1840–1893)

La donna è mobile

from *Rigoletto*

originally for voice and orchestra

Giuseppe Verdi
(1813–1901)

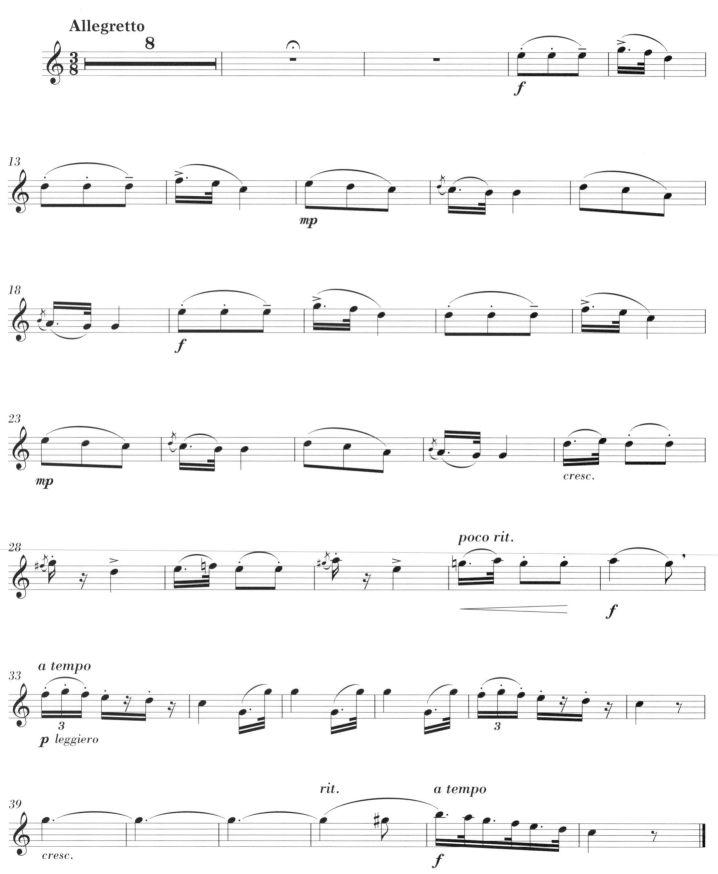

CONTENTS
BY COMPOSER

Minuet in D minor

from *Notebook for Anna Magdalena Bach*, BWV Appendix 132

originally for keyboard

Anonymous

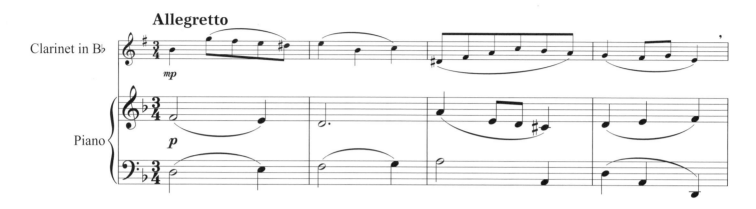

Musette in D Major

from *Notebook for Anna Magdalena Bach*, BWV Appendix 126

originally for keyboard

Johann Sebastian Bach
(1685–1750)

Adagio
Op. 63, No. 24
originally for clarinet and piano

Carl Baermann
(1811–1885)

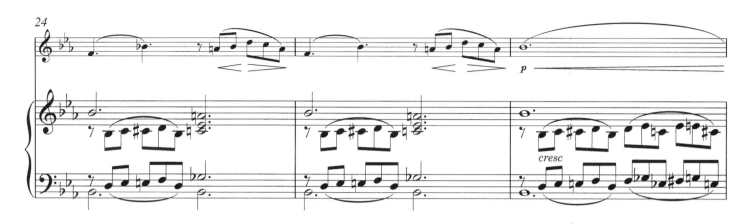

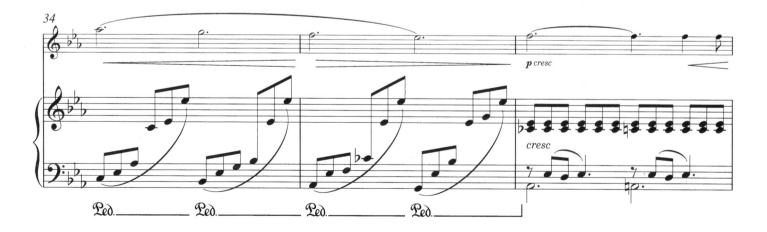

Schlummerlied
Op. 84, No. 2
originally for clarinet and piano

Carl Baermann
(1811–1885)

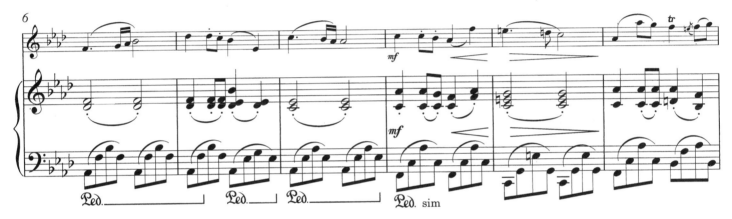

Marmotte
from *Eight Songs*, Op. 52, No. 7
originally for voice and piano

Ludwig van Beethoven
(1770–1827)

Minuet in G Major

from *Six Minuets*, WoO 10, No. 2

originally for piano

Ludwig van Beethoven
(1770–1827)

Tempo di Minuet

Ode to Joy
from Symphony No. 9 in D minor, Op. 125
originally for chorus and orchestra

Ludwig van Beethoven
(1770–1827)

With spirit

Toreador's Song
(Votre toast, je peux vous le rondre)
from *Carmen*

originally for voice and orchestra

Georges Bizet
(1838–1875)

Minuet
from String Quintet in E Major, Op. 11, No. 5
originally for string quintet

Luigi Boccherini
(1743–1805)

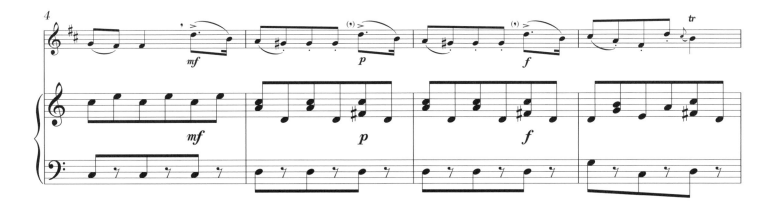

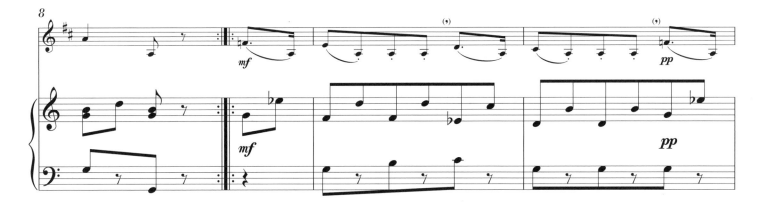

*Ornaments are optional.

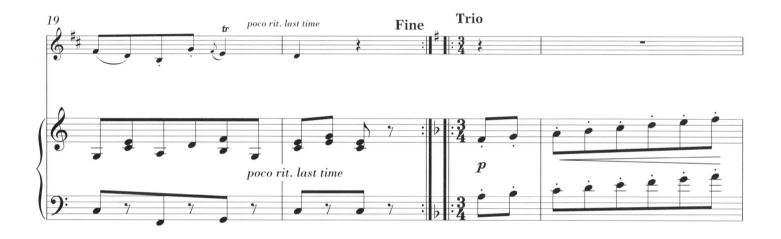

D.C. al Fine

Hungarian Dance No. 5

originally for piano duo

Johannes Brahms
(1883–1897)

Poco più mosso

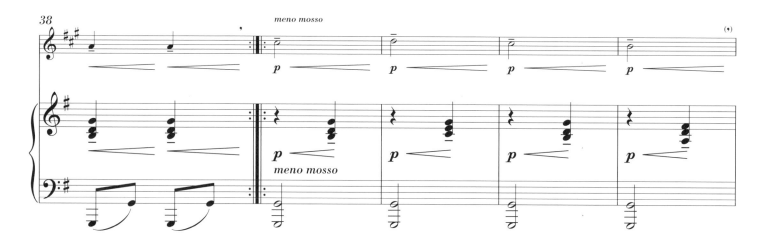

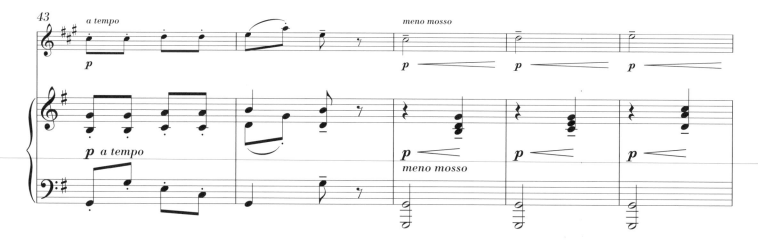

D.C. al Coda (no repeats)

CODA

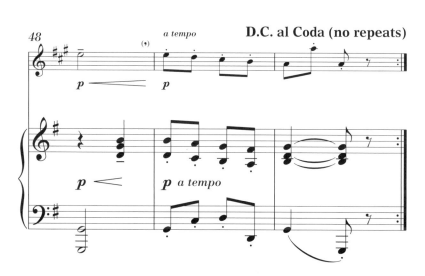

Intermezzo
Op. 117, No. 17
originally for piano

Johannes Brahms
(1883–1897)

Un poco più andante

Waltz
Op. 39, No. 15
originally for piano

Johannes Brahms
(1833–1897)

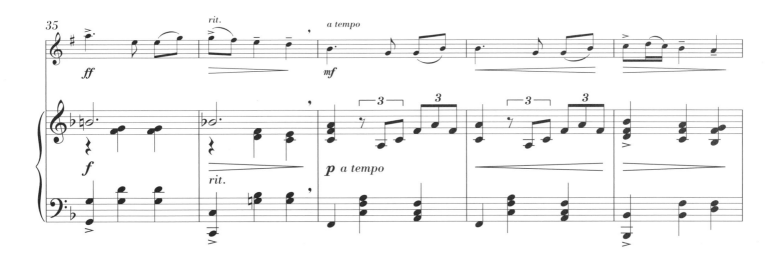

Lullaby

Op. 49, No. 4

originally for voice and piano

Johannes Brahms
(1833–1897)

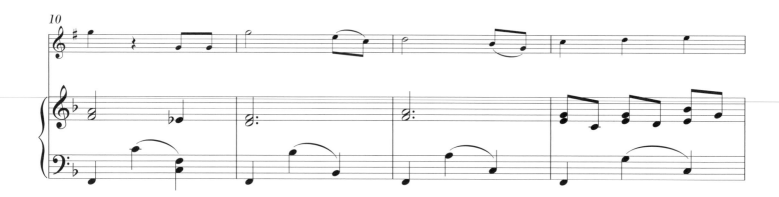

Etude in E Major
Op. 10, No. 3
originally for piano

Frédéric Chopin
(1810–1849)

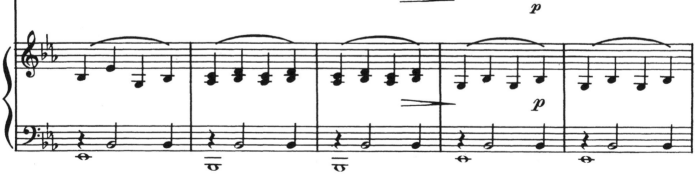

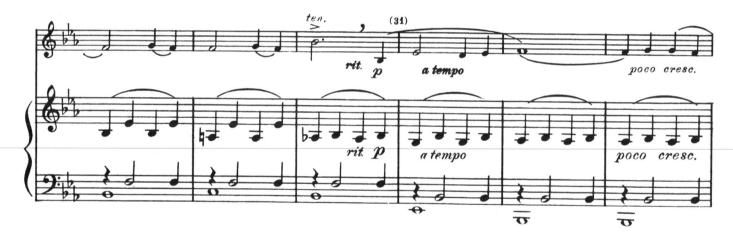

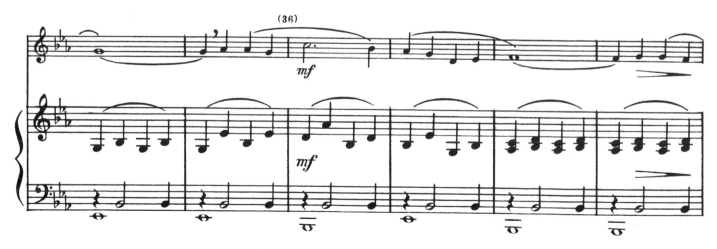

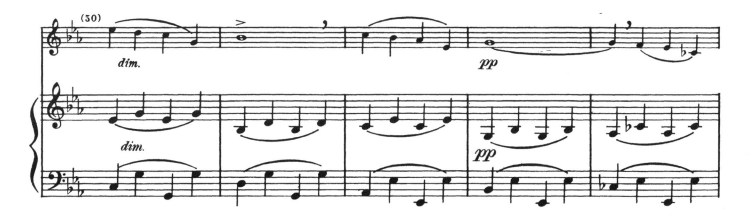

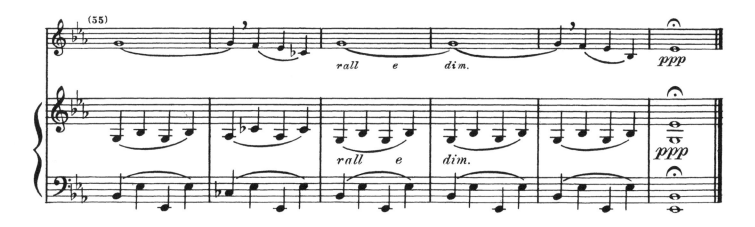

Largo

from Symphony No. 9 in E minor, Op. 95 "From the New World"

originally for orchestra

Antonín Dvořák
(1841–1904)

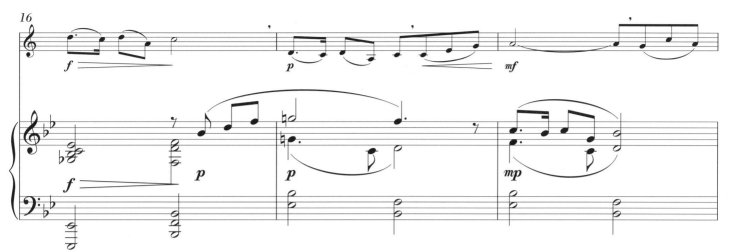

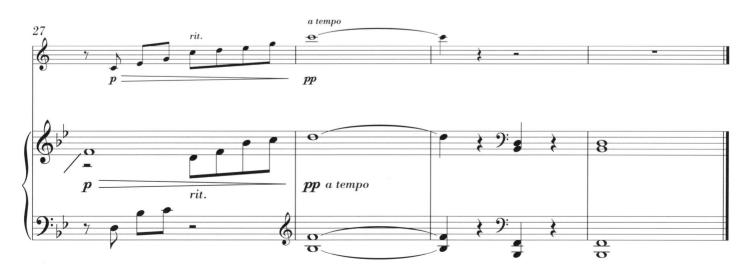

Pomp and Circumstance
March No. 1
originally for orchestra

Edward Elgar
(1857–1934)

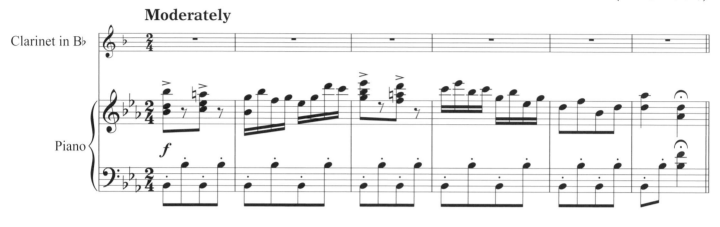

Pavane

Op. 50

originally for piano

Gabriel Fauré
(1845–1924)

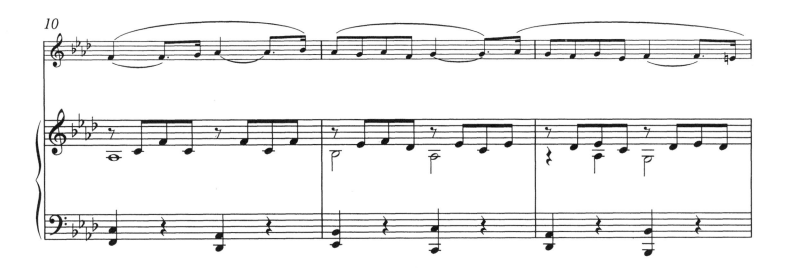

19

22

D.S. al Coda

CODA

molto rit.

Irish Tune from County Derry

originally for piano

Percy Grainger
(1882–1961)

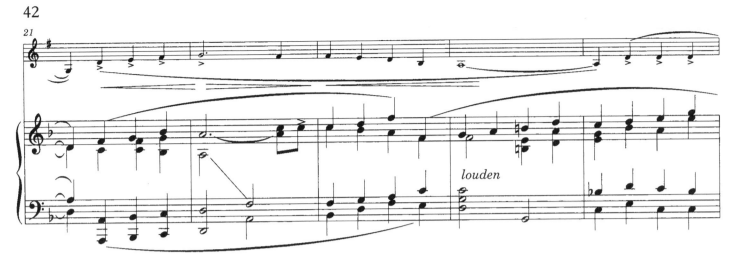

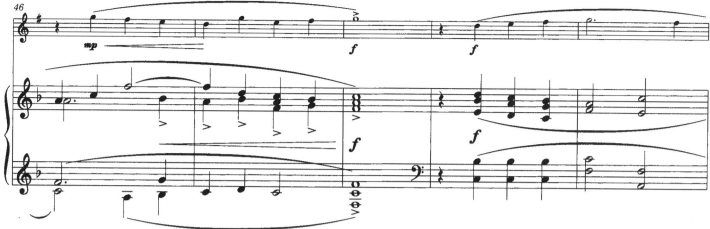

Mazurka in C minor

originally for piano

Mikhail Glinka
(1804–1857)

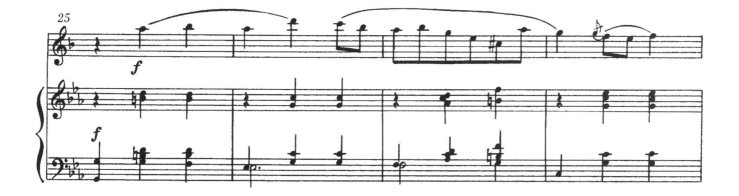

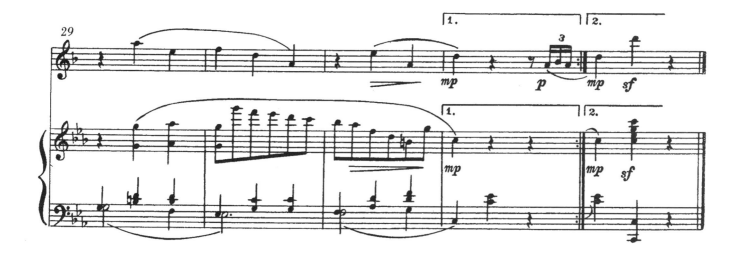

Dance of the Blessed Spirits

from *Orfeo ed Euridice*

originally for orchestra

Christoph Willibald Gluck
(1714–1787)

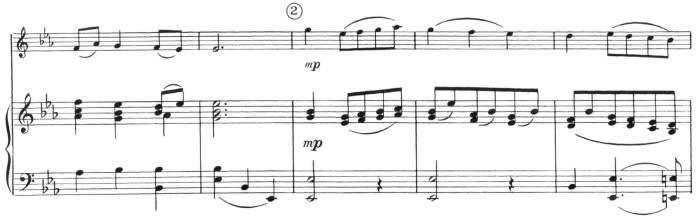

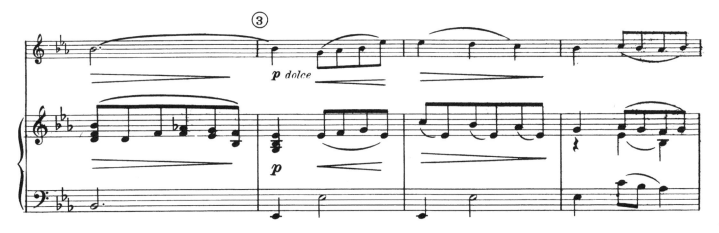

Funeral March of a Marionette

originally for piano

Charles Gounod
(1818–1893)

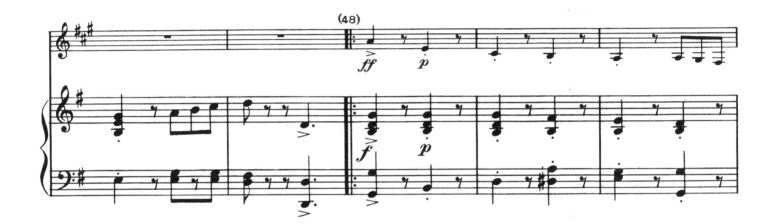

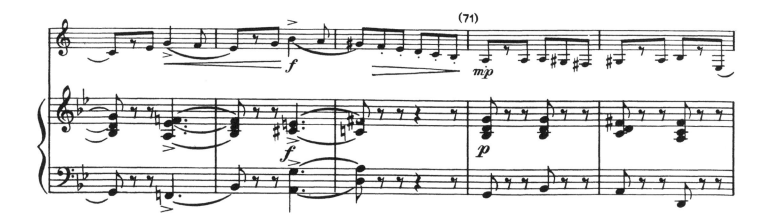

Solvejg's Song

from *Peer Gynt*

originally for orchestra

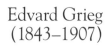

Edvard Grieg
(1843–1907)

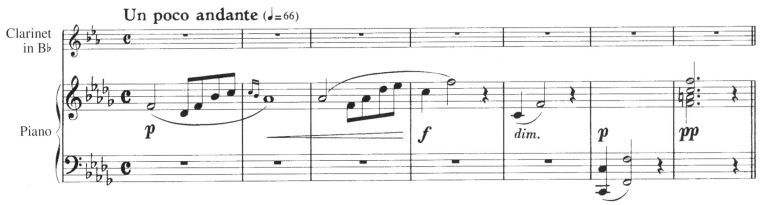

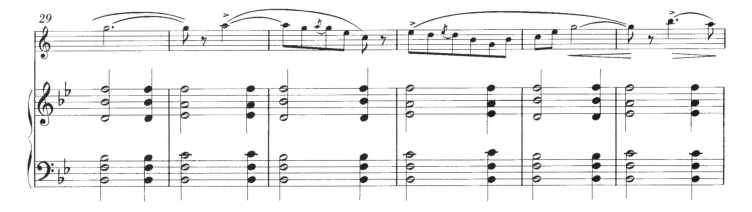

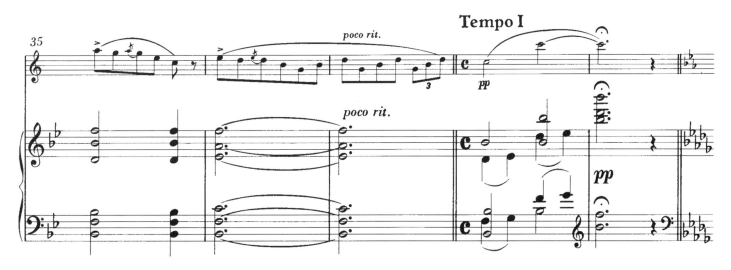

Aria con Variazioni
from Suite in B-flat Major, HWV 434
originally for keyboard

George Frideric Handel
(1685–1759)

Clarinet
in C

Piano

He Shall Feed His Flock

from *Messiah*

originally for voice and orchestra

George Frideric Handel
(1685–1759)

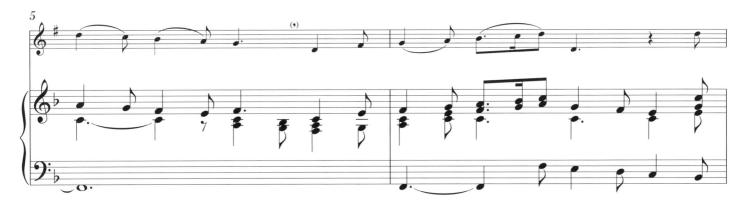

Largo

(Ombra mai fù)

from *Serse*, HWV 40

George Frideric Handel
(1685–1759)

Andante
from Symphony No. 94 in G Major "Surprise"
originally for orchestra

Franz Joseph Haydn
(1732–1809)

St. Anthony Chorale

originally for chamber ensemble

Franz Joseph Haydn
(1732–1809)

Clarinet in C

Piano

Jupiter Chorale

from *The Planets*

originally for orchestra

Gustav Holst
(1874–1934)

Andante maestoso

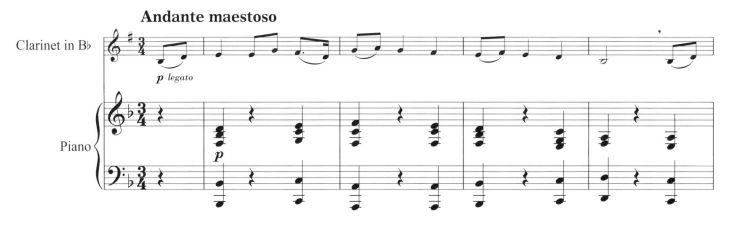

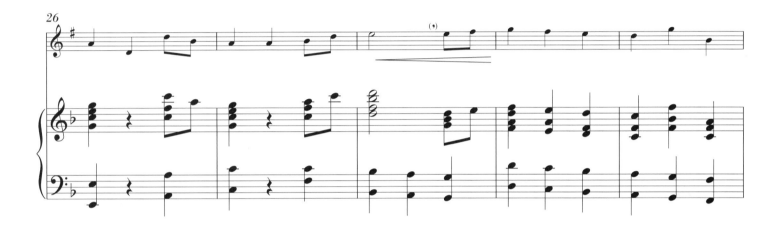

Evening Prayer

from *Hansel and Gretel*

originally for voices and orchestra

Engelbert Humperdinck
(1854–1921)

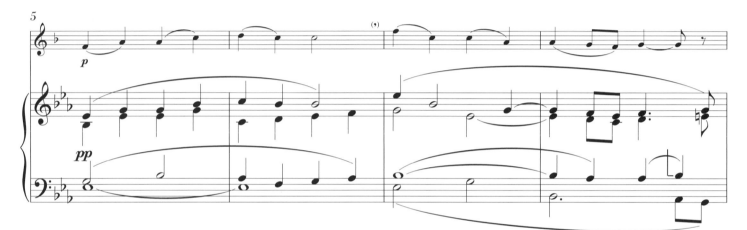

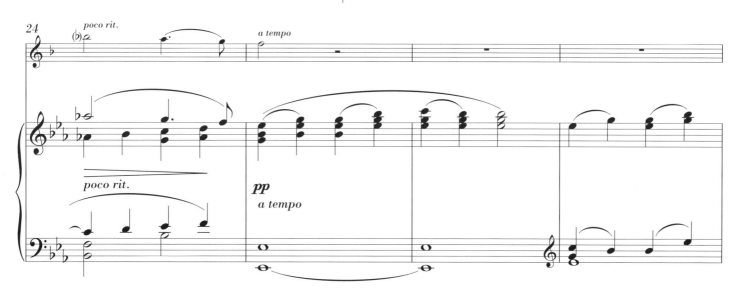

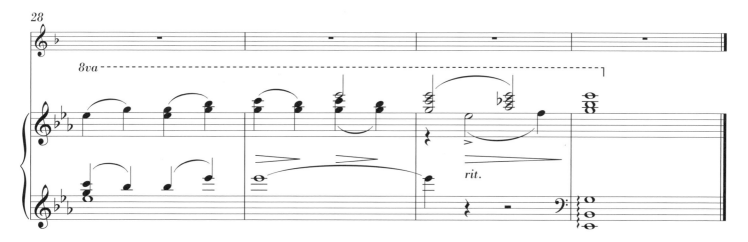

Waltz
from *The Merry Widow*
originally for orchestra

Franz Lehár
(1870–1948)

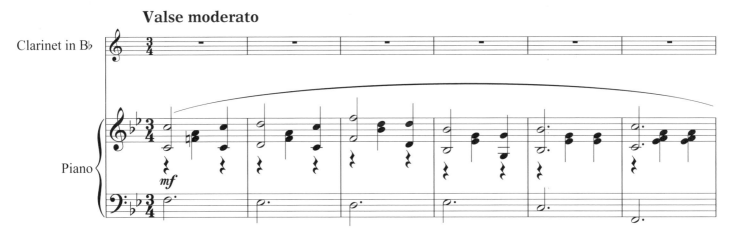

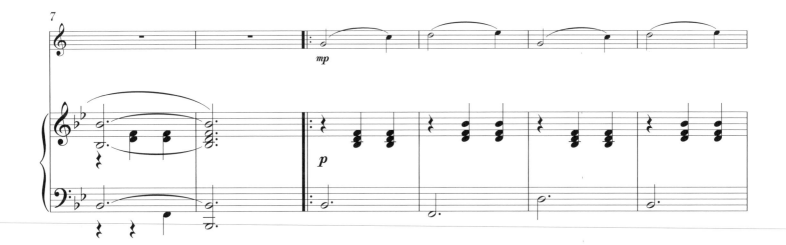

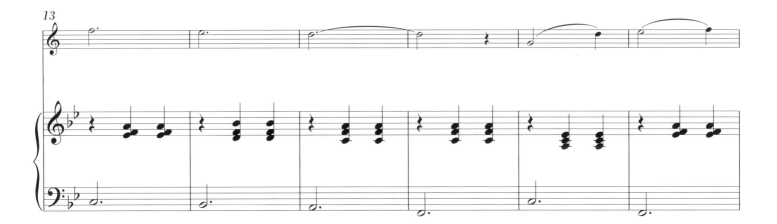

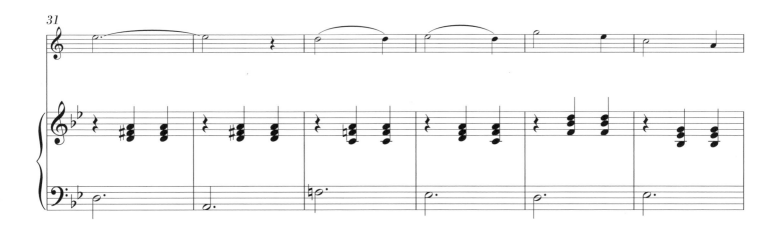

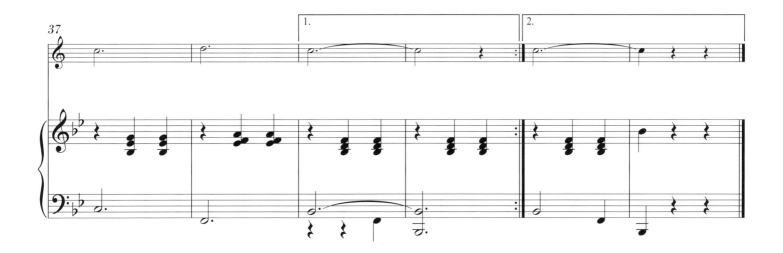

Non più andrai

from *The Marriage of Figaro*

originally for voice and orchestra

Wolfgang Amadeus Mozart
(1756–1791)

Barcarolle
from *The Tales of Hoffmann*
originally for voices and orchestra

Jacques Offenbach
(1819–1880)

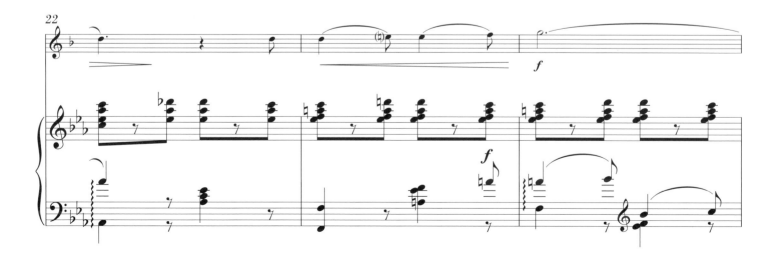

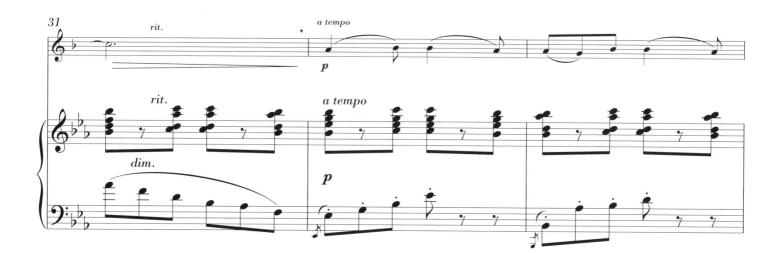

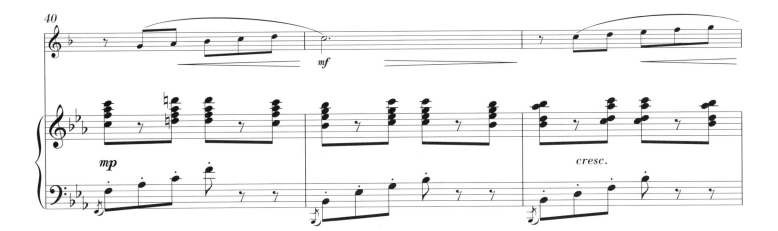

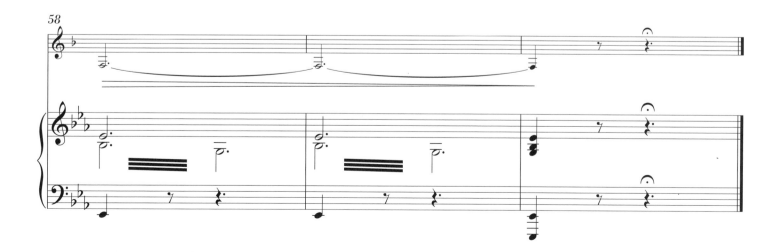

Canon
(Canon in D)
originally for 3 violins and basso continuo

Johann Pachelbel
(1653–1706)

O mio babbino caro

from *Gianni Schicchi*

originally for voice and orchestra

Giacomo Puccini
(1858–1924)

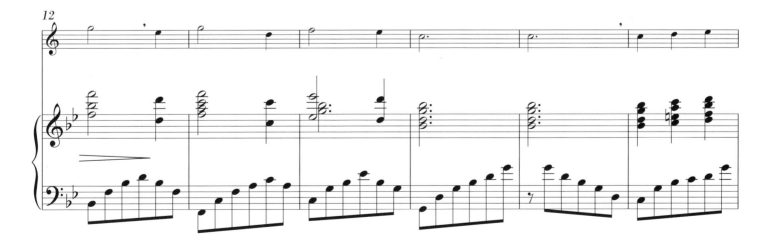

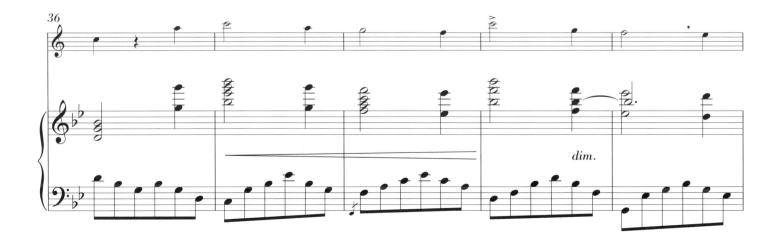

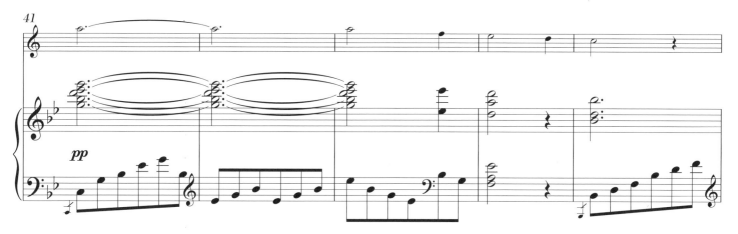

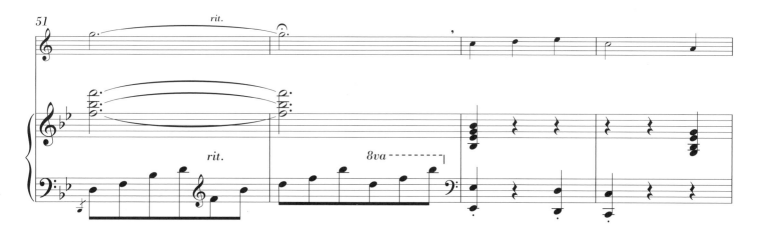

Minuet in G Major

from *Notebook for Anna Magdalena Bach*, BWV Appendix 114

originally for keyboard

Christian Petzold
(1677–1733)

Da Capo al Fine

Minuet in G minor

from *Notebook for Anna Magdalena Bach*, BWV Appendix 115

originally for keyboard

Christian Petzold
(1677–1733)

Da Capo al Fine

Ave Maria
originally for voice and piano

Franz Schubert
(1797–1828)

Sehr langsam

Clarinet in B♭

Piano

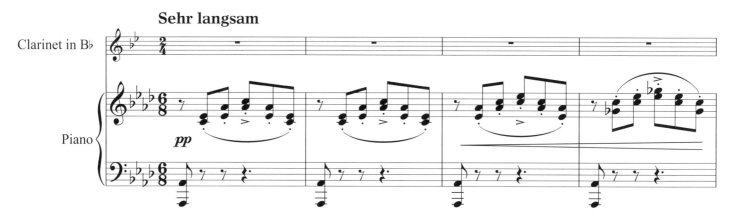

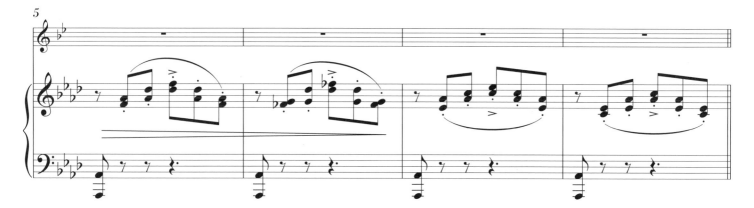

Heidenröslein
Op. 3, No. 3
originally for voice and piano

Franz Schubert
(1797–1828)

Lullaby
Op. 92, No. 2
originally for voice and piano

Franz Schubert
(1797–1828)

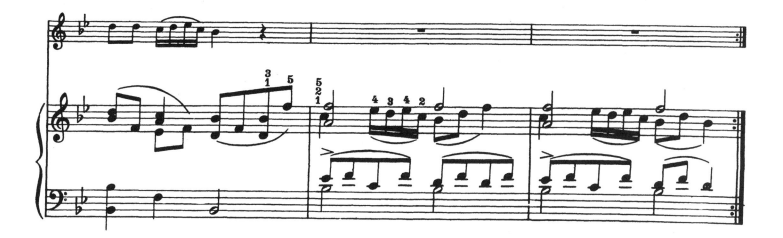

To Music
(An die Musik)

originally for voice and piano

Franz Schubert
(1797–1828)

Moderately

About Strange Lands and People

from *Scenes from Childhood*, Op. 15, No. 1

originally for piano

Robert Schumann
(1810–1856)

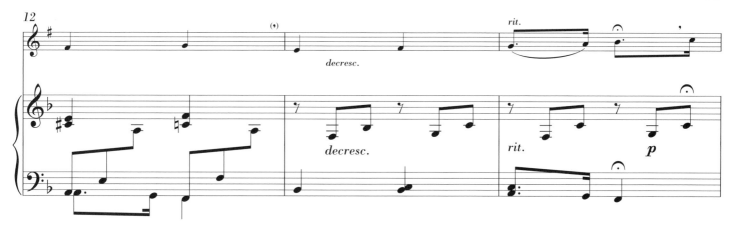

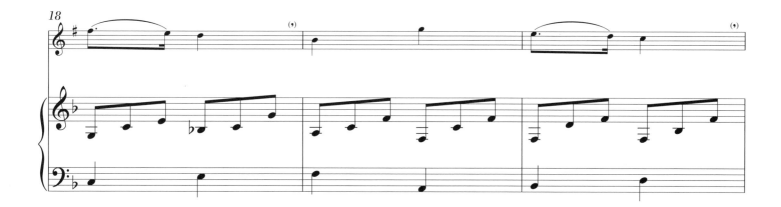

The Merry Farmer

from *Album for the Young*, Op. 68, No. 10

originally for piano

Robert Schumann
(1810–1856)

Brisk and Lively

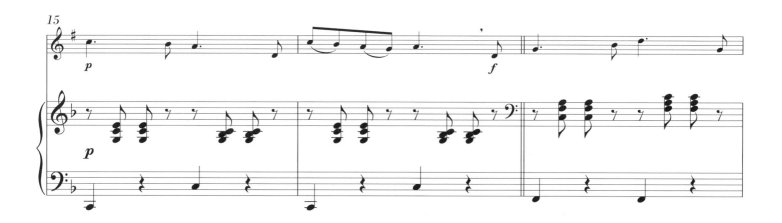

Wild Horseman
(Wilder Reiter)
from *Album for the Young*, Op. 68, No. 8
originally for piano

Robert Schumann
(1810–1856)

The Moldau
from *Ma Vlast*
originally for orchestra

Bedřich Smetana
(1824–1884)

Allegro commodo non agitato

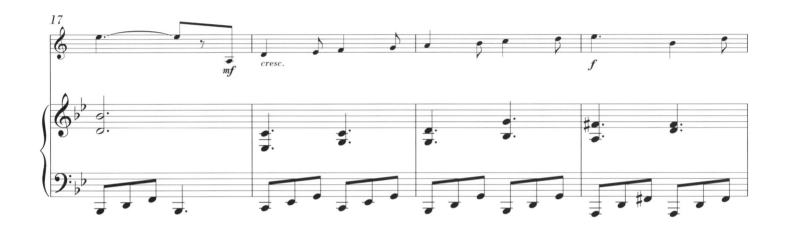

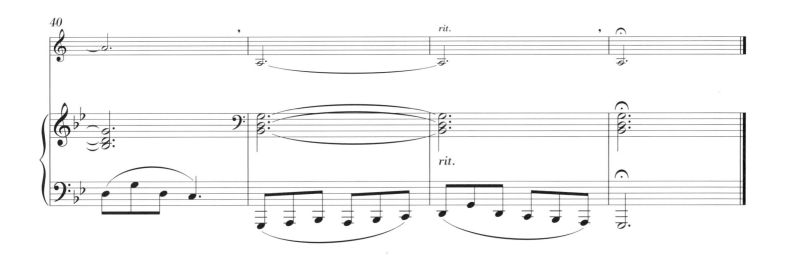

Emperor Waltz

originally for orchestra

Johann Strauss II
(1825–1899)

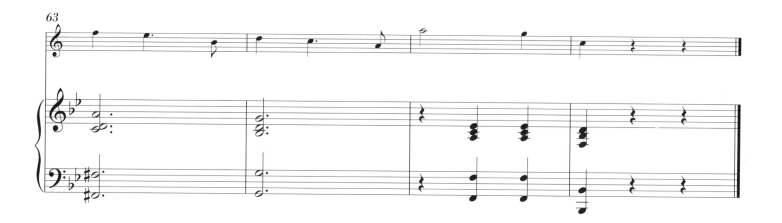

On the Beautiful Blue Danube

originally for orchestra

Johann Strauss II
(1825–1899)

D.S. al Coda

CODA

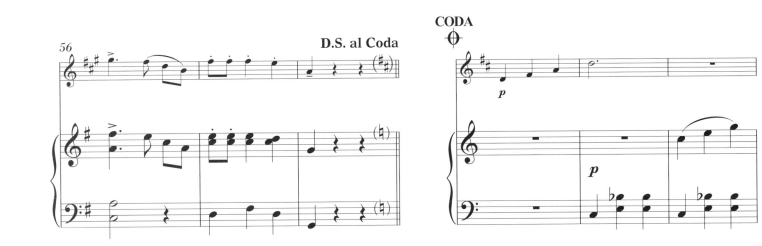

Theme
from *Swan Lake*
originally for orchestra

Pyotr Il'yich Tchaikovsky
(1840–1893)

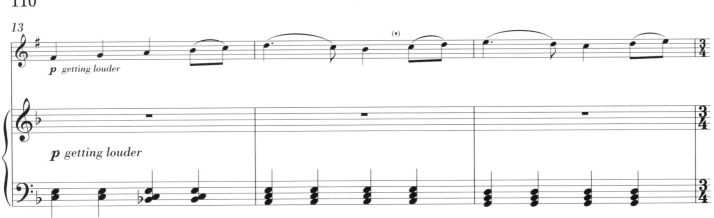

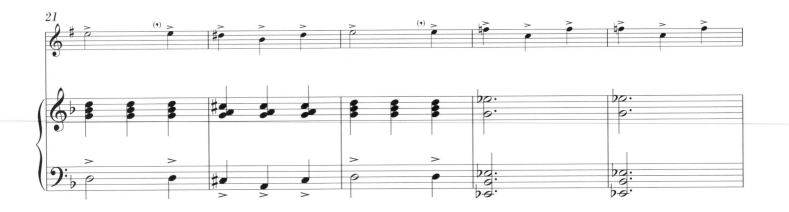

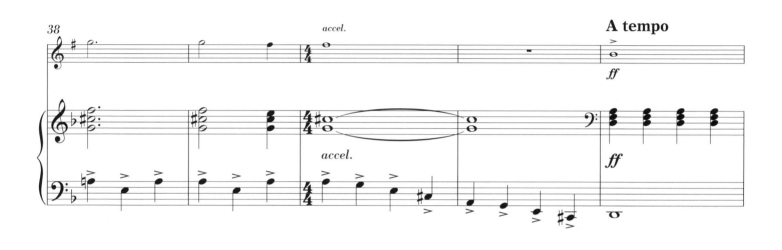

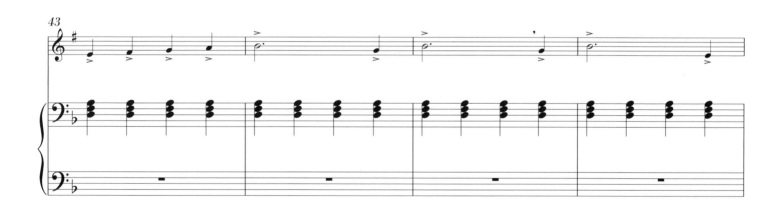

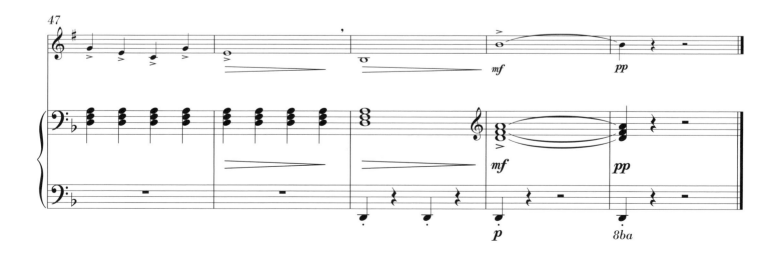

Andante

from Symphony No. 6 in B minor, Op. 74
"Pathétique"

originally for orchestra

Pyotr Il'yich Tchaikovsky
(1840–1893)

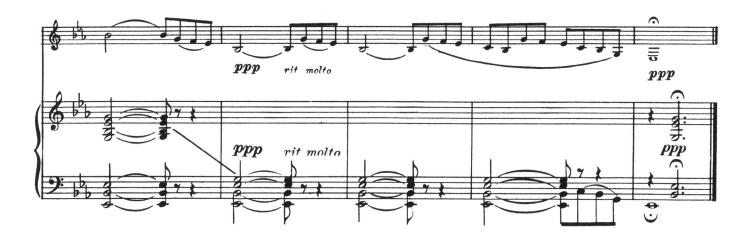

Waltz
from *Sleeping Beauty*
originally for orchestra

Pyotr Il'yich Tchaikovsky
(1840–1893)

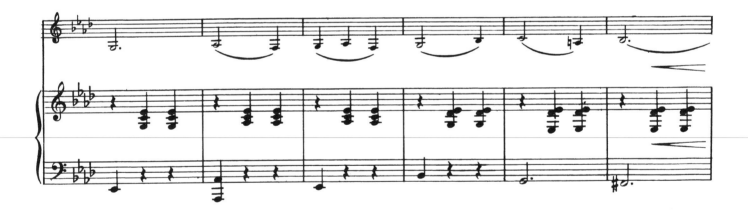

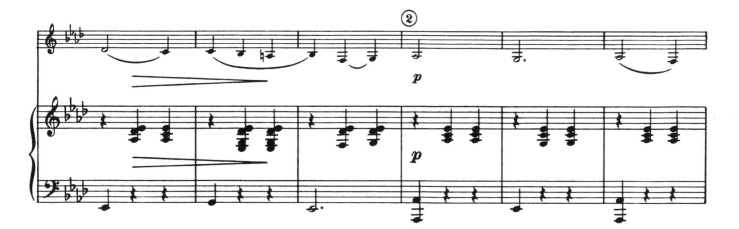

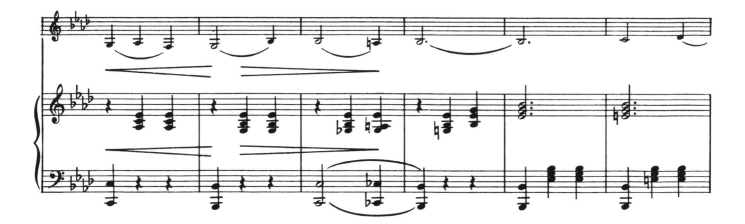

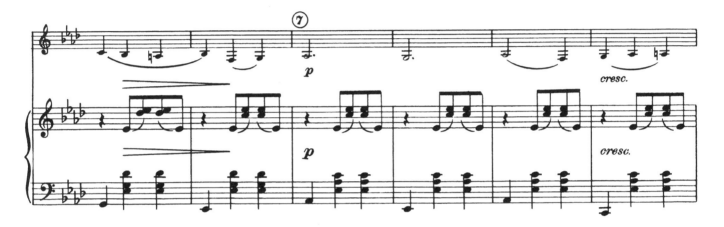

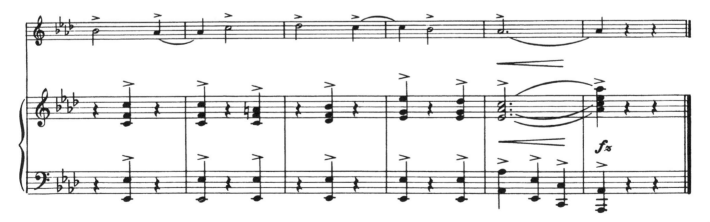

La donna è mobile

from *Rigoletto*

originally for voice and orchestra

Giuseppe Verdi
(1813–1901)

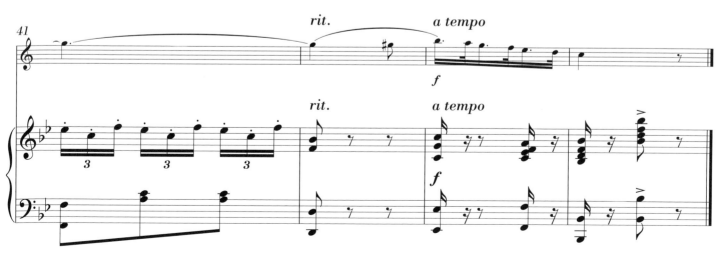